Conter

4   About the authors
6   Our sponsors
7   Acknowledgments
8   Foreword

11 SECTION 1
    Introduction

15 SECTION 2
    A Chair for all seasons
    Stages in the Chair-CEO relationship

21 SECTION 3
    Finding a balance

24 3.1 Operational boundaries:
    Helicopter view or close involvement?
26 3.2 Access and availability:
    Flexible or fixed?
28 3.3 Default mode:
    Challenging or supportive?
30 3.4 Who leads:
    Chair or CEO?
32 3.5 Managing disagreement:
    Air differences or present a united front?
34 3.6 Forming a view:
    Dependent or independent?
36 3.7 Representing the organisation:
    Chair or CEO?
38 3.8 Friendship:
    Help or hindrance?
40 3.9 Convergent or divergent perspectives?
42 Have you struck a good balance?

45 SECTION 4
    Know yourself

45 Emotional Intelligence
46 Insights from psychoanalysis
    and neuroscience
48 Transactional analysis
50 Strategies for action

53 SECTION 5
    When things go wrong
    What are your options?

57 SECTION 6
    Insights from research

57 An overview of the literature
57 How do we judge a
    Chair-CEO relationship?
58 What helps achieve a good
    Chair-CEO relationship?
60 What hinders?
61 Approaches to managing
    this relationship

65 SECTION 7
    Further resources and reading

69 SECTION 8
    Conclusions

71 SECTION 9
    List of interviewees

About the authors

Ruth Lesirge

Ruth Lesirge has 35 years' experience of work within the public and third sectors. She is an experienced voluntary sector leader, and former charity Chief Executive. She is the Chair of the Association of Chairs, a trustee of London Film School and Bishopsgate Institute and a former Vice Chair of ACEVO. Ruth served on the ACEVO Governance Commission in 2013. Before working in the non-profit sector she was Principal of an adult and community education service.

Ros Oakley

Ros Oakley has 25 years' experience in leadership, management and policy roles in the sector and as a consultant to non-profit organisations. With Ruth she co-founded the Association of Chairs, and is now its first Executive Director. She is also a principal consultant with Cass Centre for Charity Effectiveness. She has an MBA from London Business School. Ros was previously Chair of the board at Charities Evaluation Services.

Ruth and Ros wrote the Association's first publication *A Chair's Compass*. They have worked together on many governance projects including co-authorship of the *Good Practice in Trustee Recruitment* toolkit, running a mentoring scheme for Chairs for the Governance Hub, developing an online board appraisal toolkit for the website KnowHowNonProfit and helping to deliver the Cass Centre for Charity Effectiveness board development programme for Help the Hospices – which entailed working with 63 different hospice boards. Their careers have enabled them to observe at first hand scores of non-profit Chair and Chief Executive relationships.

The development of this guide

There is already some guidance on the Chair-Chief Executive relationship. Notably some useful resources from ACEVO which we refer to in SECTION 7.

We did not however find a guide looking at this important relationship from the Chair's perspective.

We started by reviewing what others had written. We are particularly grateful to Hilary Barnard for conducting a review of the academic literature for us (which we publish on our website). We compared what we read with our own experience and those of others with whom we have worked and extensively discussed these issues. We felt there was much sound advice, but also some important gaps. For example, there was scant exploration of the psychology that is involved in this important relationship. Our next step, with the help of colleagues, was to conduct 22 interviews with Chairs and Chief Executives. We are grateful to them for their insights. You can read about our interviewees in SECTION 9.

Finally we draw on our own Chair-Chief Executive relationship. Writing the guide has helped us reflect on how we work together and identify the strengths and areas for development.

Our sponsors

CCLA

CCLA is one of the UK's largest charity fund managers. For over 50 years they have provided competitive and attractive investment services that help clients achieve their aims. CCLA's products and services have a strong long-term record, are fairly priced, managed responsibly and in a manner consistent with the ethics of their clients. CCLA's staff understand the particular needs and challenges of charities and public sector organisations. CCLA's ownership ensures stability and independence. CCLA Investment Management Limited and CCLA Fund Managers Limited are authorised and regulated by the Financial Conduct Authority.

CCLA

Odgers Berndtson

Odgers Berndtson is the UK's pre-eminent executive search firm, helping private and public sector organisations find the highest calibre people for permanent Executive and Board appointments in the UK and internationally.

With the largest specialised Not-For-Profit team in the UK and access to the networks of our specialist search teams across all sectors we have developed a significant track record of advising, supporting and sourcing Chairs and trustees of Not-For-Profit organisations. Our experience with both Chief Executive and Chair selection enables us to help organisations find complementarity and effective leadership.

Acknowledgments

First and foremost
We would like to thank our sponsors whose funding has made this guide possible. We are very grateful to **CCLA** and in particular to **Michael Quicke** and **Andrew Robinson** whose early and consistent support has been invaluable to the Association of Chairs. Similarly we are grateful to **Odgers Berndtson** and in particular to **Julia Oliver** who has been steadfast in her support for our organisation.

We thank all our interviewees both those listed in SECTION 9 and those who remain anonymous.

We thank also:
Hilary Barnard for so helpfully preparing a literature review.
Martin Farrell (Get 2 the Point) and **ACEVO** for sharing his insights from supporting CEOs referred from ACEVO's CEOs in Crisis service.
Linda Laurance for her advice on mediation.
Marcus Page for stimulating our thinking on self-awareness.
Sam Younger for his helpful comments on our draft.

We are grateful to the following who contributed in a variety of ways:
Helen Baker, Margaret Coleman, Danny Curtin, Stephen Goldman, Alice Maynard, Neil Morrick, Derek Twine, Rebecca Weinberg, Jacqueline Williams and John Williams.

And finally we thank all those Chairs, Chief Executives and trustees who have shared ideas and experiences with us, helping to shape our thinking.

Foreword

As I know from personal experience, the relationship between the Chair and the Chief Executive matters. A strong relationship helps an organisation thrive, a poor one has the potential to do real damage. Achieving the right balance in the relationship is not straightforward and as this guide makes clear, there is no easy formula or single solution. That's why both Chair and Chief Executive must recognise both the importance of their relationship to the health of the organisation and the need to invest in making it work.

Despite our aspirations to do the job well, most of us who are Chairs and Chief Executives need help and support from time to time. ACEVO has a long-established track record of supporting Chief Executives, including the small number of executive leaders who find their relationship in crisis. The Association of Chairs was launched two years ago and is developing a range of support services specifically for Chairs; we at ACEVO welcome this.

The Association has already established a reputation for high quality events and publications. And I am pleased to welcome this new addition, a thought-provoking guide focused on the Chair and Chief Executive relationship, looking at the relationship from the Chair's unique perspective.

A Question of Balance poses good questions for Chairs to consider, including some to discuss with their Chief Executive, and provides pointers for strengthening and developing the relationship including signposts to relevant resources.

ACEVO and the Association of Chairs share a common goal – that of fostering strong executive and non-executive relationships and continually developing the quality of the sector's leadership.

Paul Farmer
CHAIR ACEVO, CHIEF EXECUTIVE MIND

INTRODUCTION
SECTION ONE

Introduction

The relationship between the Chair and the CEO is pivotal to the functioning of your charity or non-profit organisation.

A successful partnership provides the organisation with clear and effective leadership, promotes trust and confidence internally and externally, enabling effort to be focused on the charity's purpose.

The relationship is often rewarding, energising and enables both parties to give their best. It is also a lynchpin for the wider relationships between the board and staff.

If you and your CEO are not able to work together, the impact will reverberate throughout the organisation, diverting energy and dissipating focus. A failing relationship can create havoc for the organisation. Strained relationships keep both Chairs and CEOs awake at night and create difficulty for all those who need to navigate around the tensions. For CEOs such difficulties are potentially career threatening. Even where there is no crisis in the relationship, both Chairs and CEOs often find it a challenge to forge a relationship that brings out the best in them both.

Experienced Chairs recognise that they need to invest time in working with and getting to know the CEO to become a cohesive 'top team'. They explore what they each value, seek to understand each other's strengths and weaknesses, and build trust. They understand the importance of integrity, honesty and consistency in behaviour.

There is no single right or easy way to manage the relationship. It's worth recognising that this relationship is unlike any other. There are inherent tensions and it is complex. The key challenge for the Chair in the relationship with the CEO is balancing what seem to be contradictory approaches. For example, you need to balance freedom for the CEO and accountability to the trustees; support and challenge; being strategic and the ability to home in on details when necessary; and the executive and the non-executive perspective.

There may be a big disparity in your professional or leadership skills and experience, or in your specialist knowledge. The relationship needs to be flexible to take account of the unique circumstances and personalities of those involved, as well as the needs of the organisation you both lead. It is also likely to change over time, perhaps imperceptibly, requiring frequent rebalancing.

We believe Chairs need to recognise and accept their responsibility for making a success of the relationship. To play your part you need to be willing to reflect on what you do and the impact your approach has on others. And be willing to change.

There may be things about your CEO that you find difficult and would wish to change – but changing others is notoriously difficult. We think a more helpful starting point is to consider what you can change about yourself. The choice to change ourselves is within our control; it can also be a catalyst to change in your CEO and others.

Our aim then is to help you reflect on the relationship you have with your CEO. Whether you are a new Chair or an experienced Chair, we encourage you to consider what you currently do, the implications of your approach, other possible alternatives and ask yourself whether change on your part could help you build a stronger relationship, one that better serves your organisation's purpose.

Our guide offers a number of ways for you to explore the relationship you have with your CEO and includes these sections.

Stages in the Chair-CEO relationship
Here we outline stages in the relationship and highlight some fundamental things you will want and need to have in place.

Finding a balance
In this key section, we identify nine common themes in the Chair-CEO relationship and explore contrasting approaches and the associated strengths and weaknesses. We invite you to consider the balance you have struck and the implications of your choices.

Know yourself
We present some frameworks to explore the factors that may affect your behaviour as a Chair.

When things go wrong
This provides some high level pointers for those who are experiencing difficulty in their relationship with their CEO.

Insights from research
In this section we summarise themes and findings from some of the existing research and writing about this key relationship.

Further resources and reading
We highlight existing resources and materials that will enable you to pursue the ideas and themes discussed.

You may wish to read the whole guide from end to end or dip into the sections that interest you most.

There are some aspects we do not cover in detail as we believe they are worthy of separate, in-depth attention, notably recruiting your CEO, remuneration, appraising your CEO and your legal obligations as an employer.

A good relationship with your CEO is not an end in itself. As we outline in A Chair's Compass, this is just one part of the Chair's role. It is, however, a key contribution to the ongoing success of the organisation.

Finally, we do not think this guide is either the first word or the last word on this important topic. We look forward to hearing and exchanging perspectives that enable us to deepen and improve relationships between Chairs and CEOs.

A CHAIR FOR ALL SEASONS
SECTION TWO

A Chair for all seasons

STAGES IN THE CHAIR-CEO RELATIONSHIP

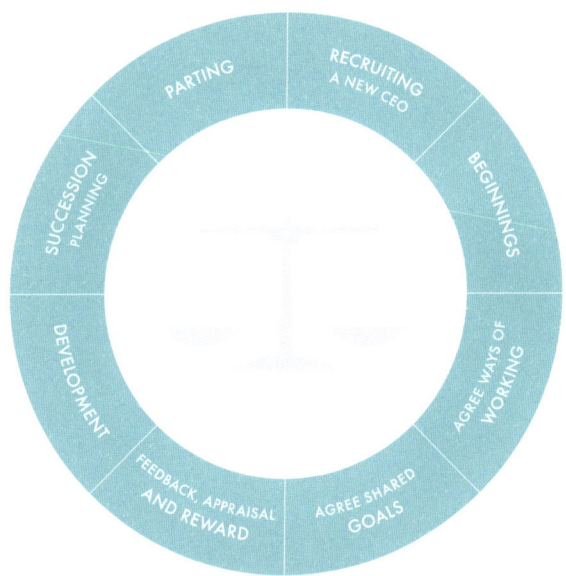

As with all relationships, each one will have its own path and momentum; that's what makes it fascinating but demanding.

There are however predictable stages in the relationship, and there are some core policies and practices that help the relationship. We summarise these below and highlight key things to have in place. We hope it provides a useful checklist for you. If you do not have these in place, it's worth asking – why not? In most cases useful practical resources have already been developed which we list in our *Further reading and resources* section.

RECRUITING A NEW CEO

THINGS TO THINK ABOUT

What learning can you bring from the relationship with the outgoing CEO?

Are you clear about the key priorities for the incoming CEO?

Are you asking for a big change? If so, are you prepared to back the CEO through the rough as well as the smooth?

No one is perfect – are you equally aware of your new CEO's strengths and their weaknesses? Have you worked out how to compensate for the latter?

Are you casting the net widely enough in looking for your next CEO?

Are you recruiting in your own image?

WHAT TO HAVE IN PLACE

Clear description of the CEO's role.

Recruitment policy.

Appropriate HR procedures including grievance and disciplinary procedures.

Access to specialist independent HR advice for the board (as needed).

Ideas about the shape of your regular supervision/support meeting.

BEGINNINGS

THINGS TO THINK ABOUT

When either of you is new in post devote more time to meeting and communicating.

Try to understand each other's motivations and build trust.

Have some social time together.

WHAT TO HAVE IN PLACE

A well thought through induction programme.

Consider and discuss joint Chair-CEO training that can explore (and refresh) mutual understanding.

AGREE WAYS OF WORKING AND KEEP THEM UNDER REVIEW

THINGS TO THINK ABOUT

What are your preferred ways of communicating and meeting?

How do you make it 'safe' for your CEO to admit mistakes and share bad news?

Explore assumptions (see next section).

Aim for an environment where you can sound each other out confidentially.

WHAT TO HAVE IN PLACE

Undertake a simple role analysis of who does what. Focus on the priorities for the next 6-12 months.

Delegated authority policy setting out matters reserved to the board, committees, to the CEO and staff.

A plan (developed together) of what the board will address in the next 12-18 months.

AGREE SHARED GOALS

THINGS TO THINK ABOUT

Direction and priorities.

Reviewing progress.

WHAT TO HAVE IN PLACE

Schedule of meetings to agree objectives and review progress.

Agreed ways of assessing progress.

FEEDBACK, APPRAISAL AND REWARD

THINGS TO THINK ABOUT

Give regular motivating feedback.

Agree a clear and fair appraisal process.

Ensure performance is recognised and rewarded appropriately.

If there are problems, find a timely way to have the difficult conversation.

WHAT TO HAVE IN PLACE

A process for both regular meetings and a more formal appraisal – preferably annual.

A remuneration policy.

DEVELOPMENT

THINGS TO THINK ABOUT

Discuss professional development in relation to the needs of the organisation and the CEO.

Consider membership of ACEVO for your CEO.

Mentoring and coaching.

WHAT TO HAVE IN PLACE

A budget for training and development for CEO and yourself.

SUCCESSION PLANNING

THINGS TO THINK ABOUT

How to develop the wider team.

Potential for internal succession without making promises about future appointments.

WHAT TO HAVE IN PLACE

Training and development policy.

Succession policy.

PARTING

THINGS TO THINK ABOUT

Recognise the achievements of your CEO.

What you and the organisation can learn, especially if things have not gone so well.

Ensure the reputation of the organisation is managed with a clear message about the departure of the CEO.

WHAT TO HAVE IN PLACE

An exit interview with the CEO.

Put good HR processes and access to specialist advice in place in advance, when there is no problem, so that they are available if required. Where the parting is not amicable it's vital to have this.

These stages assume it is the CEO who is new in post. If it is you, the Chair who is new to the organisation, think through your own induction. Consider how you will get up to speed with the work of the organisation, its context and the key stakeholders that you want to meet. Bear in mind the arrival of a new Chair can be an unsettling time for a CEO.

In addition to working out how the two of you will work together, think through how you will work with the members of the board and the management team (if there is one).

Agree how contact with staff will work. You don't want to meddle, but you need to be aware of the organisational culture and the health of relationships within it. It's a good idea to make this part of an appraisal process, but consider additional ways in which you can hear staff views, formally and informally. Is there a whistleblowing policy in place?

The board needs to be aware of the progress of your relationship with the CEO, and know about their performance. There are a variety of ways you might achieve this. If you have a Vice Chair they might be involved in the appraisal of the CEO; you could have regular trustee-only time at your board meeting when you update the board on the CEO's achievements and any challenges. And consider what routes are open to you and your CEO if there is a breakdown in your relationship.

See also SECTION 5, page 53

FINDING A BALANCE
SECTION THREE

Finding a balance

Every Chair-CEO relationship is unique, moulded by their particular personalities and histories as well as the particular context of their board and organisation.

And the relationship is not a static one; it evolves over time and in response to changing circumstances.

Essentially it's a question of balance.

A little like a surfer, the Chair (together with your counterpart the CEO), has to keep shifting position on the surfboard to ride the changing contours of the wave and avoid crashing down. It's exhilarating when you get it right – and can feel overwhelming when you don't. And, of course, you don't control the waves.

Exactly how you get the balance right will be up to you. There are, however, recurring themes about what needs to be balanced. In this section, we have identified 9 different dimensions of the relationship, which we think are important for you to think through.

For each dimension we have identified two ends of a spectrum of practice. You may find that in some cases you operate at one end of the spectrum. In others you may take a mid-point. There is no 'right answer'. A range of different approaches are both appropriate and legitimate. The most important point is not the position you take on the spectrum, but the consequences of taking that position. To help you reflect we have identified strengths and weaknesses associated with the ends of the spectrum.

We hope this section will enable you to consider your own approach, to compare it with others and to understand the potential impact of what you do on your CEO and on the organisation.

HOW TO USE THIS SECTION

For each of the dimensions we suggest that you reflect on these three areas.

Where you think you are on the spectrum?

Why? For example is that a conscious choice, personal preference or an accident of history?

What are the strengths and weaknesses of the approach you and your CEO currently have?

At the end of the section we make some recommendations about exploring the dimensions with your CEO.

You can use these dimensions at any point in your relationship. We think these explorations are particularly important when the relationship is new or undergoing significant change.

A QUESTION OF BALANCE: SECTION 3

SECTION 3.1
OPERATIONAL BOUNDARIES – HELICOPTER VIEW OR CLOSE INVOLVEMENT?

The board is ultimately responsible for the charity but typically devolves responsibility for its operations to staff. There is no universal rule about where the boundary between governance and operations lies. It will be shaped by the context of your organisation, its stage of development and its staffing. Some areas will be clear – others less so.

Experienced trustees and Chairs are adept at holding the balance, recognising that what is unwelcome interference when the organisation is on an even keel, can be seen as essential in a crisis or if resources are stretched.

Oversight and supervision by the Chair during the development of a high risk project can be experienced by the CEO as over-anxious meddling when appropriate risk management and reporting processes are in place.

Taking responsibility for an area of operational work can be particularly helpful where there is very limited capacity, but it requires an agreement that in this regard only, the Chair is accountable to the CEO (while in governance mode it's the other way round). It may not be an easy separation of roles for either party. But if you can achieve this, you may find it's a productive way for the Chair and CEO to work, and develops understanding of each other's style and pace.

Agree your roles on key issues such as strategy development, how you prepare together for board meetings, the extent of the Chair's involvement in developing board papers, and communicating with staff.

Another issue is, once you've agreed boundaries, how fixed or flexible are they?

....

"There are times when you need to step in, for example if the team aren't handling it or aren't telling the truth. You have to be like a bird of prey: you hover and then occasionally you have to deep dive, when you need to. You have to have enough knowledge of the organisation to do the job properly."
BERYL HOBSON

....

"Most difficult is when a well-meaning Chair doesn't understand the boundaries between ops and governance."
NIGEL CHAPMAN, EXPERIENCED CEO

....

"I remember once over-stepping the mark and became inappropriately involved in operational matters... It was reassuring that she and I could address it." CAROLE EASTON

....

HELICOPTER VIEW

POTENTIAL ADVANTAGES	POTENTIAL DISADVANTAGES
Helps you to hold the long-term view; you may be less easily diverted by the urgent.	You may end up being too remote to grasp the realities of the organisation.
You're less likely to step on each other's toes.	This position may be inappropriate to the size or context of your organisation.
It reduces uncertainty about leadership domains internally and externally.	It may be an excuse to mask unwillingness to give time or engage with the demands of the role.
You can make good use of your complementary and differing perspectives.	You are so removed from the detail your CEO feels unsupported or you are unable to hold them to account.

POTENTIAL ADVANTAGES	POTENTIAL DISADVANTAGES
You are well placed to assist in an emergency.	It can impair your ability to hold the strategic overview.
You achieve a deep understanding of the operational demands and dilemmas.	You may undermine the CEO and senior team and erode the authority and distinctive profile of the CEO.
The operational capacity is extended.	Closeness can blur lines of accountability.
Your CEO regards you as accessible.	Your organisation may become over-dependent on you; which makes leaving and succession planning more difficult.
Your expertise is available to staff.	

CLOSE INVOLVEMENT

Where on this spectrum is your relationship with the CEO?
What would your CEO say?

SECTION 3.2
ACCESS AND AVAILABILITY – FLEXIBLE OR FIXED?

Good, honest communication is crucial – but how do you make that happen – and fit it around your other commitments? The time commitment required of Chairs is often under-estimated. And there is a wide range of assumptions about the degree of access CEOs will have to their Chairs. Aim to find a way of working that keeps you in good contact, helps you to have in-depth conversations about significant issues, ensures 'no surprises' for either party and allows quick responses when needed. Some like to have a fixed schedule and 'rules', others are more ad hoc.

The specific combination of face-to-face meetings, Skype, email, phone and text exchanges will vary. Some schedule monthly or bimonthly meetings, a weekly call, with agreement on interim contact. Some specify hours when they are or are not available or when the contact needs to be different, for example no emails or calls after a particular hour; use text for urgent matters. It helps to match the nature of the contact to what it is you want to discuss. Take care with email – it's all too easy to seem abrupt or lacking in empathy; resulting in indignation, anger or confusion. The permutations are unimportant provided they work for you both.

The mirror image of this is also critical; will your CEO take your calls if they come at weekends? It may be the only time you have, but possibly their only time off. And how quickly do you both expect a response to emails?

Finally, sort out why you are making contact in advance of the call or email. Know what you want, be insightful about the needs of your CEO and reach agreement.

"With experience, I have learnt to be more swift to raise key issues that will impact negatively on the organisation and its internal culture. It's critically important to avoid fear, prevent surprises and promote a culture of honesty." DEREK TWINE

"It's important to discuss how we will communicate. We discuss what is important for the CE to tell me and what I expect to hear – and it's not just a question of 'keeping the Chair happy'. I make it clear that I am available at any time, not necessarily just when there is a crisis, but when the CE needs 'to talk'." SARAH PHILLIPS

"When things have gone wrong it's often because the Chair has been cavalier about it. You need to know the central significance of this relationship and act as if you know that." MARTIN FARRELL

FLEXIBLE
ACCESS AND AVAILABILITY

Your CEO feels supported. You can move in quickly and help in a crisis or sudden opportunity. It creates a habit and culture of shared problem-solving. You are routinely informed and up-to-date.	Easy availability creates over-dependence on you and the role. It feels like a burden to be Chair. You set a difficult precedent for your successor. You may be encouraging a just-in-time approach. You may blur the operational/governance boundaries.
POTENTIAL ADVANTAGES	**POTENTIAL DISADVANTAGES**
It makes space for the CEO to operate. Your time together is more focused and strategic. It helps you maintain useful distance from the day-to-day. It discourages from the start any inclination to be over-involved.	You can be too aloof and distanced by the boundaries set. Your knowledge of the challenges faced is not deep enough. There is insufficient time allocated to build your relationship and trust. Email traffic between you replaces good qualitative exchanges.

FIXED
ACCESS AND AVAILABILITY

Where on this spectrum is your relationship with the CEO?
What would your CEO say?

SECTION 3.3
DEFAULT MODE: CHALLENGING OR SUPPORTIVE?

Chairs need both to challenge and to support, but what is the balance? And what is your default position? Some Chairs shy away from challenge because they find it uncomfortable, with the result that issues are allowed to fester or escalate to the detriment of the charity. Others may be inclined to challenge and neglect the need to encourage. What is regarded as a healthy, constructive challenge by one person may be regarded as aggressive and adversarial by another.

It's also a question of temperament – yours and that of your CEO. Robust challenge is part of the professional toolkit for some; others may find it contrary to their own preferences. Positive, energetic challenge may well be welcomed, but also has the potential to inhibit or destroy confidence, making able people wilt.

Chairs have been perceived as rude, abrasive or aggressive when they believed what they were offering was a useful, challenging inquiry. The key point is that our temperament and ability to manage ourselves are critical in helping to grow and stabilise this important relationship.

It can help to adopt a coaching approach, encouraging creativity and empowerment. This involves asking open questions about the 'why' and 'how' of the issue being addressed. Seek to help the CEO to think more broadly, explore scenarios and options before taking action. The ambition is always to mine the CEO's skills and knowledge, and help them explore opportunities that are beyond the 'same old solutions'.

See also page 51

"When the balance between support and challenge is out of kilter it's like being 'in shark-infested waters' – it's most dangerous when the CE has no sense of where the Chair is on a key issue." NIGEL CHAPMAN, EXPERIENCED CEO

"The organisation needs to know that the Chair is holding the CEO to account." DAVID FRENCH, EXPERIENCED CEO

"I'm a first-time Chair and my relationship with the new CEO wasn't easy; asking questions provoked negative and defensive responses. I've found it very demanding to work out how to support and motivate him and keep the charity on the rails." CHAIR

"I feel very comfortable taking strong action with a failing CEO because I've done it before." CHAIR

CHALLENGING

Difference can promote debate and contribute to rigorous decision-making.

It may make it easier for you and your board to name and tackle poor performance.

You know how to stretch the CEO and hold them to account.

Challenge can engender a culture of questioning.

Being constantly challenged is wearing for CEO and can be uncomfortable.

It may inhibit openness, especially when there are difficulties.

It may not bring out the best in your CEO; they may view your approach as negative criticism.

POTENTIAL ADVANTAGES | **POTENTIAL DISADVANTAGES**

It feels comfortable and confirming and may bring out the best in your CEO.

You create a sense of team in good and bad times.

It can be helpful in weathering long-term difficulties together.

Trust develops, knowing that neither of you will 'hang the other out to dry'.

There may not be enough challenge in your exchanges.

There is a risk that you prioritise the relationship over issues that need to be tackled.

Being very bonded may create neediness.

SUPPORTIVE

Where on this spectrum is your relationship with the CEO?
What would your CEO say?

SECTION 3.4
WHO LEADS – CHAIR OR CEO?

Chairs and CEOs are by role (and often by temperament too) leaders. Some aspects of their roles may be clearly delineated – for example that the Chair has the authority on behalf of the board to hire and fire.

Others need to be negotiated. Sometimes they achieve a happy equilibrium, in other cases one of them is clearly leading.

You may have become Chair with a strong and charismatic executive leader in post, whose contribution has defined the organisation. The challenge in that case is to celebrate and support their talents without relinquishing the necessary governance oversight.

It requires a clarity about your role and early negotiations with your counterpart about how you plan to deliver on it.

The worst consequence for the organisation is where either the Chair or CEO is disproportionately dominant with a resultant loss of confidence in one or both of you, and/or a failure to fulfill your role.

Conversely a new Chair may feel they have a mandate to sort out a struggling organisation and then acts too quickly, failing to work in tandem with the CEO and leaving the trustees behind.

The question of who leads on what will inevitably reflect your respective needs and talents; at best it will be informed by being perceptive and a generosity of spirit towards your CEO.

Whatever balance you strike, it needs to be in the best interest of the organisation and its mission.

"Sadly there are sometimes egos at play. I have seen chief executives completely ignored by a board Chair. An over dominant chief executive is a real problem, but so too is an over dominant chair." CHAIR

"As Chair, you have to leave your ego at the door. People's opinions are not right simply because of their role." CHAIR

"Sometimes the Chair's summary of a board discussion has felt more like a summary of her views, and that is difficult to challenge." EXPERIENCED CEO

"Do not allow others on the board to act as if they are the Chair. It's like an imbalance on a boat – it puts it out of kilter." MARTIN FARRELL

CHAIR LEADS

POTENTIAL ADVANTAGES	POTENTIAL DISADVANTAGES
Where CEO is not a natural leader, you may be filling a gap.	Such an approach can undermine the authority of the CEO.
It can result in a strong strategic long-term focus.	You may encroach on and limit the CEO's room for manoeuvre.
Trustees may respond well to such board-level leadership and engage.	Your work may be resented by senior staff.
It can be seen as ensuring accountability.	Your trustees may back off and defer to you.
You fulfil your potential and are useful.	It may result in too much power being vested in one person.
	You may not have the professional credibility your CEO does.
Conventional and reassuring for trustees and external stakeholders.	A very strong CEO can result in a lack of challenge, with Chair and board merely rubber stamping decisions.
The operational focus of the CEO enables consistent and steady progress.	Your organisation becomes over-dependent on its CEO.
Enhances CEO credibility and ability to harness their networks.	There is too much power vested in one person.

CEO LEADS

Where on this spectrum is your relationship with the CEO?
What would your CEO say?

SECTION 3.5
MANAGING DISAGREEMENT – AIR DIFFERENCES OR PRESENT A UNITED FRONT?

One of the reasons for becoming Chair is commitment to the cause the organisation is addressing. However, as many of us have found, Chairs' and CEOs' views may diverge on matters of strategy, policy and the politics, even though we may want the same long-term outcomes.

Some Chairs may feel they need to screen their trustees from differences they have with the CEO. They may believe that the board is relying on harmony in the top team and that morale or confidence would be lost if trustees knew about disagreement on an important issue. If you and your CEO are in agreement it's worth asking how and when do you enable the board to contribute different perspectives and to be appropriate partners in the decision-making.

Other Chairs believe it is a good thing for important differences of opinion to be aired with the trustees and that it adds vigour to the board's debate. If that is your position, be clear about the potential outcomes and how you plan to get to a decision. One approach for big strategic issues is to stage the discussion over several meetings starting with a wide ranging discussion of principle and moving over time to a narrower set of options.

If there are big differences and especially if other staff are present, ensure the discussion does not undermine the authority of the CEO with his or her team and enable the board to feel that such differences are productive and manageable. You will need to gauge when the time for disagreement is over and trustees must make a decision.

Consistency of message by both of you may not be a major issue when in calm waters, but can be critical in difficult times or when your organisation is of interest to the media. At this point Chair and CEO must be able to respond together, offering the same key messages and speaking as one.

"It's important to 'out the elephant in the room' and deal with difficult differences even if you're not sure of the outcome."
JULIA LEVER

"It's best to work out disagreements in private to begin with. If you really do have differences, make it clear that although you disagree you haven't fallen out and provide support for each other's viewpoints. If there's no mutual respect it's not going to work." BERYL HOBSON

"I wish I'd had some help to work out how to deal with the disagreements between me and my CEO – and the tensions that caused within the board." CHAIR

PRESENTING A UNITED FRONT

POTENTIAL ADVANTAGES	POTENTIAL DISADVANTAGES
It is helpful and reassuring to the board.	The default position for both is unexamined agreement with each other.
Together you give a clear, unambiguous lead both internally and externally.	You may be unpractised and less deft at negotiating when you disagree.
You can be resilient to attempts to 'divide-and-rule'.	As a top team you seem to be unassailable.
The ability to speak with one voice is helpful in dealing with serious challenges.	Decisions seem pre-agreed and may close down debate by trustees.
It may help others to reach a shared view quickly.	It limits your ability to encourage challenge at board meetings.

POTENTIAL ADVANTAGES	POTENTIAL DISADVANTAGES
This can stimulate productive debate.	Robust challenge can be experienced as bullying
Your relationship is creative, generating constructive tension.	Your behaviour may be disconcerting to trustees and other stakeholders
Working together is exciting and promotes curiosity about the other's position.	It can slow down decision-making.
A 'third way' is more likely to emerge.	There can be a reputational risk to the detriment of your organisation.

AIRING DIFFERENCES

Where on this spectrum is your relationship with the CEO?
What would your CEO say?

SECTION 3.6
FORMING A VIEW – DEPENDENT OR INDEPENDENT?

Many Chairs bring highly relevant experiences and knowledge about the organisation's field of activity, or about running an organisation. However, this is usually a part-time, voluntary role alongside often full-time staff and CEO.

These circumstances mean that retaining an independent view can be demanding and sometimes unsuccessful. The result can be that Chairs and their boards come to rely entirely on their CEO for information and advice about the external and the internal context.

The concept of independence is an important one for Chairs, given the board's responsibility for ensuring the best interests of the organisation. Independence of thought is also an asset when major decisions are needed or when the board is tackling a complex and difficult decision. Your role is to help trustees interrogate the issues, test the propositions presented and form a coherent view. A confident CEO will respect such insights and fresh strategic thinking.

It is, therefore, important that alongside the central guidance and information from CEOs, Chairs seek out independent sources of information and advice when appropriate, taking care to justify this and the choices they make on external sources. This is not intended to diminish the role of the CEO, although it has been evident in a few cases that Chairs have been poorly advised or at worst manipulated and deceived.

Maintaining independence of view can be demanding on the Chair, CEO and their relationship. The best Chairs accept that some degree of tension is inherent but work to manage it. One Chair told us how helpful it was to hear from the Chairs of sub-committees the perspectives of other staff.

Staff surveys and 360 degree reviews of senior staff can also offer perspectives on the health and culture of your organisation, as can appropriate participation in a staff conference.

"It's such a pleasure talking to someone who's an expert in their field (when you're not) and learning from her." GERALD OPPENHEIM

"Part of my role is to be a facilitator and help other trustees confront (rather than avoid) what needs to be confronted." JULIA LEVER

LARGE DEGREE OF DEPENDENCE ON CEO

It may result in less investigative work for you.

Data sources arrive having been filtered for quality and relevance.

You can be confident that the initial analysis of information has been done.

The CEO's skills are used and validated.

You and the board receive a pre-filtered view.

The CEO has more power in shaping or influencing your view.

There is a risk of missing significant sources of information.

There may be a risk of being misled or deceived.

POTENTIAL ADVANTAGES	POTENTIAL DISADVANTAGES
You are well positioned to garner a greater diversity of view. It promotes governance independence. You can draw on the knowledge and networks of trustees and others. It leads to more rounded interrogation of the options. Trustees do their own 'sense-making' of context and options.	The CEO's contribution may be devalued or set aside. Other perspectives may not take proper or sufficient account of organisational context. The information received may be of variable quality. It may imply a lack of trust in your CEO.

LARGE DEGREE OF INDEPENDENCE FROM CEO

Where on this spectrum is your relationship with the CEO?
What would your CEO say?

SECTION 3.7
REPRESENTING THE ORGANISATION – CHAIR OR CEO?

Bearing in mind the best interest of the organisation and its mission, it is worth asking who is best placed to represent the organisation. Profile gives CEOs more access to influencers and decision-makers. It may also be motivating to feel that their professional profile is being developed within their day job.

At the same time, some Chairs speak with the affinity of personal experience about the cause, for example, the Chairs of some hospices and disability charities. On other boards, the Chair is selected or elected because of their professional expertise or the roles they play in other parts of their lives, for example, as a leader in an area of medical research.

These additional dimensions are potentially a huge asset. Where the Chair has acknowledged deep and specialist knowledge and is a public figure, they may be the best choice. For example, a distinguished and well-known actor speaking on behalf of a theatre project.

However, representing the organisation also requires other skill sets and aptitudes. These include up to date knowledge, grasp of key facts, understanding of the politics, availability and ability to put across the organisation's messages convincingly. These are more often found in the CEO role description than the Chair's. In addition it is often the CEO who has had recent relevant training such as media skills.

These are not necessarily either/or choices; representing the organisation can be shared providing you have sorted out what special brief each of you will hold. You or your CEO may have particular sensitivities about status or reputational ambitions and these may unwittingly surface. Others of us will be content or indeed relieved to be the backroom person and proud of their partner's ability to face outwards on behalf of your organisation.

Finally, we highlight the danger of being lulled, flattered or hijacked into making statements beyond your remit or knowledge and creating a reputational risk. Planning how to deal with any fall-out in case of such a scenario is helpful.

"Our CEO generally fronts public events; I top and tail the formalities if appropriate, but we are flexible and sort it out on a case by case basis."
PELHAM ALLEN

CEO SPEAKS FOR THE ORGANISATION

Chair is not competing with CEO.

Your CEO is usually best placed to initiate or respond – especially at short notice.

You do not have to be a good public speaker.

You can still discuss and prepare together.

You may not be seen to be publicly accountable.

CEO feels unsupported.

Your absence may be criticised by stakeholders, particularly in a crisis.

You may be less motivated to keep abreast of potential vulnerabilities.

POTENTIAL ADVANTAGES	POTENTIAL DISADVANTAGES
You can extend the organisation's capacity for getting media profile. It can be a demonstration of governance commitment and add to the status of the role and individual. It offers you learning opportunities and you may enjoy the activity. You can share the strain with the CEO. You may be best placed to speak on the issue.	Your CEO may feel excluded, under-valued or resentful. You may not have sufficient information to do the role well. Chair may not be regarded externally as the appropriate spokesperson. It may undermine the credibility of your CEO.

CHAIR SPEAKS FOR THE ORGANISATION

Where on this spectrum is your relationship with the CEO?
What would your CEO say?

SECTION 3.8
FRIENDSHIP – HELP OR HINDRANCE?

There are a range of views about when, how and to what extent friendships enhance or distort good governance and the operational leadership of the organisation. The views of most of our interviewees were summed up by the quote 'We are friendly but not friends'. But there were some who were vociferous in their condemnation and others who were convinced of its value.

In some new and young non-profit organisations, the only people prepared to support the initiative are the friends and family. This may also be the case in some charities, where they are established in memory of an individual person or to address the circumstances that caused their death.

Some Chairs interviewed made clear that part of their job satisfaction derives from their friendship with the CEO. In such cases the closeness is a given and can be an asset, or a liability.

In other settings, Chairs and CEOs who work well together may regard it as poor practice to be in any way part of each other's personal lives. The concern is that friendship impedes independence, making it hard to be critical of the CEO and make difficult decisions about their performance or their future in the organisation.

As the organisation develops and grows the extent to which friendship is appropriate may change.

"Our friendship predates us founding the charity, and is a huge strength. The high degree of trust we have in each other speeds things up and makes it easier to air differences. It's important others know we do not have blind loyalty to each other." CHAIR

"Friendship is OK as long as you can both differentiate between the roles when necessary… Perhaps better to promote friendliness, respect and courtesy." DEREK TWINE

"The Chair's job is inherently lonely. You are not there to be a friend." CHAIR

"My Chair knew my mother was dying from Motor Neurone Disease, but she never spoke of it. Not once." CHIEF EXECUTIVE

DO NOT REGARD EACH OTHER AS FRIENDS

You may find it easier to deal with difficult tasks such as CEO underperformance.

Distance from the CEO can avoid managing the more complex emotions of friendship.

Distance can help you avoid being drawn in to areas where you feel disadvantaged.

Your CEO may feel unable to show vulnerability or to ask for help.

If you are distant and undemonstrative, it is much harder to 'read' each other.

Distance can be a barrier to offering help when the other is stressed.

You may both be less inclined to make allowances for each other.

It can be read as disengagement with the role on your part.

POTENTIAL ADVANTAGES

You feel supported, comfortable and safe in good and bad times.

You are more likely to be consistently open and less defensive.

A high degree of trust may result in difficulties being tackled earlier.

You're a team, able to be more adventurous in the risks you take.

The friendship maintains motivation because working together is enjoyable.

POTENTIAL DISADVANTAGES

It may make it difficult for others to challenge either of you.

There can be an unhealthy degree of re-enforcement of your own views.

The relationship may take precedence over the needs of the organisation.

You are both more hesitant in acknowledging or addressing the other's weaknesses.

REGARD EACH OTHER AS FRIENDS

Where on this spectrum is your relationship with the CEO?
What would your CEO say?

SECTION 3.9
CONVERGENT OR DIVERGENT PERSPECTIVES?

Shared values are often discussed in the context of the organisation and how it operates. There is less discussion interestingly about the extent to which the Chair and CEO have shared values and perspectives and whether it matters.

How important is it to you that the things you hold dear are shared by your CEO? For example, if you practice a faith, does it matter that your CEO does not have the same religious views? Is the answer the same if yours is a faith-based organisation? To what extent are you drawn to people who share similar family, education and class histories and assumptions about the world? Or do you seek out people who are different to you?

If there are key organisational values that your CEO needs to share you need to make these explicit and explore them during recruitment. For example if there is a requirement for service delivery to reflect key parts of your faith or philosophy. Surfacing and negotiating other values is likely to be more complex. Your core beliefs and perspectives inform who you are. You may find the situation of differing values and assumptions stimulating and the source of learning, but it can also cause strains in the relationship.

Too much similarity is a danger – but you also need enough common ground to operate effectively. The degree of synergy or diversity to which Chairs aspire in their relationship with their CEO will differ. But if Chair and CEO conversations are to go beyond easy platitudes, they will require honest and adult exchanges. Differing life and work experiences don't necessarily result in incompatible values and beliefs, but it helps for both partners to be aware of, understand and respect each other's beliefs and value base. You may have to live with some degree of discomfort engendered by the differing values you hold.

"My Chair inhabited a different world. He was powerful, privileged and rural-based whereas I was urban, immigrant and had English as a second language. Yes we worked OK but our failure to explore the differences inhibited our relationship." CEO

"Like-minded individuals are susceptible to groupthink, and variety in age, gender, and ethnicity as well as in experience and training is needed to guard against self-confirming biases – and too easily reached consensus – that often endanger businesses." [1]

"There are often trustees who want change but can't tolerate the discomfort that inevitably comes with it." MARTIN FARRELL

DIVERGENT

Potential Advantages	Potential Disadvantages
You may stimulate a different sort of creativity together.	It is hard work to constantly justify or defend your view.
Your differences of view can stretch you, generating productive challenges.	You may be in constant low-level conflict.
The consequence may be a greater diversity of perspective.	Substantively divergent views require skilled handling by both – it may be an uncomfortable place to be.
	The situation could undermine your motivation or that of the CEO's.
	If the differences are evident, they can create warring camps/cliques.

POTENTIAL ADVANTAGES | **POTENTIAL DISADVANTAGES**

Being in agreement on most things makes for swift and easy decision-making.	In assuming your values will always be aligned you risk having blind spots; it can impair independence of judgement.
Learning to understand each other becomes easy and second nature.	You may become too complacent.
It is satisfying to have your views and judgements endorsed; morale and energy spiral up.	A closed loop between Chair and CEO discourages diversity and proper attention to mind sets.
The relationship is comfortable.	It can encourage group think on the board.
Shared thinking is helpful in dealing with an external threat or challenge.	

CONVERGENT

Where on this spectrum is your relationship with the CEO?
What would your CEO say?

HAVE YOU STRUCK A GOOD BALANCE?

We hope we have prompted you to think about different dimensions of your relationship and to reflect

- Where you are on the spectrum
- Why? For example, is that a conscious choice, personal preference or an accident of history?
- What are the strengths and weaknesses of the approach you and your CEO currently have?

Is your way of working likely to cause problems for your CEO?

We recommend you now ask your CEO to do similar and then together explore the following four questions:

QUESTIONS TO EXPLORE TOGETHER

1

Do you have a shared view on where you are in the spectrum?

2

What are the strengths and limitations of your current approach with regard to your relationship and your organisation?

3

Are there aspects of the way you work together you want to clarify or change?

4

Whatever the approach you now adopt, how will you mitigate the limitations and disadvantages?

This is not a one-off exercise. Key events in the life of the charity will mean that you need to reappraise the nature and balance of your relationship with the CEO. Perhaps the amount of time you as a Chair can give has suddenly changed, or the CEO needs to change their focus because of major strategy development, restructuring or because of external pressures such as loss of funding or a reputation crisis.

A change of either the CEO or Chair is a crucial milestone in the charity's governance, management and leadership; it's therefore vital that you revisit your assumptions and ways of working. For example, it's unwise to assume that the newcomer is going to replicate (or is able to replicate) what their predecessor brought to the relationship. They will contribute their own unique strengths.

Reviewing and rebalancing is to be encouraged – the test is always: does this help us work better, to the benefit of the charity and the people and causes we serve?

---

1 Richard D. Parsons and Marc A. Feigen – The Boardroom's Quiet Revolution, HBR, March 2014, page 102

KNOW YOURSELF
SECTION FOUR

Know yourself

We believe that one of the most important things a Chair can contribute to a healthy Chair-CEO relationship is a high degree of self-awareness.

Of course both parties contribute to the chemistry of a relationship, but the part which you are most able to influence is your own contribution.

It helps to be aware of the assumptions and preferences you bring, and the factors that may make you feel vulnerable or trigger an overreaction on your part. The more aware we are of our own emotional response, the more likely we are to recognise the emotional responses in others. This knowledge can create an environment in which both feel able to give of their best.

We set out here some frameworks and insights from psychology that we think you may find thought-provoking and helpful. For those who want to know more we provide some references for further reading.

Emotional Intelligence

Daniel Goleman popularised the idea of emotional intelligence or EQ as being important to success in different areas of our lives including decision-making and how we relate to others. Many problems stem from a failure to understand and manage emotions and we need to develop our emotional intelligence. He identified the five 'domains' of EQ as:

- **Self-awareness**
  Knowing your own emotions
- **Self-regulation**
  Managing your own emotions
- **Motivating yourself**
- **Empathy**
  Recognising and understanding other people's emotions
- **Social skill**
  Managing emotions in others.

He suggests that emotional intelligence is not static but can be nurtured and developed to help us perform better.

Insights from psychoanalysis and neuroscience

Understanding our emotions and what is going on under the surface can help us to also understand our relationship with the CEO. Emotions play a part even in the seemingly most 'rational' of relationships. Neuroscientists tell us that humans have hardwired emotional and behavioural systems, shaped by our upbringing, that govern our response to others, but only a small part of which we may be aware.

These emotions shape our relationships in ways that are automatic, but broadly predictable. The unconscious purpose of our behaviours is to help us feel safe.

A key insight from psychoanalysis is that our emotional responses are often conflicted; we have an array of psychological defences that serve to 'regulate' our anxiety and maintain our equilibrium. The defences include:

> "The most common mistake is that CEOs and Chairs avoid dealing with the problem. They do not want to address the difficult issues, because it will be uncomfortable."
>
> MARTIN FARRELL

Repression
Because of anxiety about dealing with a difficult issue, a Chair may 'forget' to raise a difficult topic with a CEO.

Denial
Similar to repression but a deeper refusal to 'accept reality' for fear we might feel overwhelmed by doing so, for example acknowledging a serious fraud or risk of insolvency.

Displacement
Rather than dealing directly with the threat, a Chair or CEO may focus on another matter entirely, that is often minor or 'safe'. So for example you may focus on the CEO's expenses when the real issue is a much more profound general lack of trust.

Projection
Projection of anxiety is commonly seen in the 'scapegoating' phenomenon. We deny personal responsibility for a problem and instead blame an individual or group. For example, sometimes it's easier for a Chair (and their board) to heap responsibility on the CEO rather than acknowledge the complexities of the situation and share responsibility for an issue. At its worst this can result in a succession of short-lived CEOs. Or it can take the form of projecting superhuman capabilities onto an individual (e.g. Chair or CEO) or working group, which allows the board to be passive and dependent. For example, the Chair can put too much confidence in the CEO and retreat from his or her responsibilities.

This can be a particular danger when the CEO is charismatic and confident and 'accepts' the projection. Although it may initially result in spectacular success it is a risky approach with potentially negative long-term consequences.

Regression and dependence
When faced with a situation that causes anxiety generated by uncertainty and helplessness about what actions are needed, the board may retreat from their roles and look to the Chair or CEO to solve the problem.

Fight or flight
This includes avoiding the matter at hand (flight) or expressing that anxiety in conflict (fight). Confusingly the fight is rarely over the real matter that has given rise to anxiety but serves to discharge aggressive feelings 'safely'. So a Chair and CEO may find themselves in conflict over a secondary issue.

Pairing
Describes both the strong pull for individuals to 'find someone like me' in any group where the membership is too full of 'unknowns' and also to find a pairing that provides safety through mutual assurance. Friction between the Chair and CEO may provoke anxiety in other trustees.

All human beings use the defences above; the extent to which these mechanisms are triggered depends on the degree of anxiety we feel. Being able to identify anxieties within the relationship (both your own and those of your CEO) can help Chairs to manage the partnership productively.

Transactional analysis
Transactional analysis is a system for analysing communication between people, focusing on the dynamics in people's interactions.

> "My Chair's philosophy was that in this relationship, Chair equals Parent and Executive equals Child. And this just didn't work with a competent Executive team." EXPERIENCED CEO

A central assumption is that we have learned to behave in certain ways and may have become 'stuck' or programmed to repeatedly respond in those ways.

Eric Berne describes three modes of behaviour ("ego states") that are used by us all: Parent, Adult, and Child[2]; these are largely shaped by our early experiences:

---

2 *Games People Play: The Psychology of Human Relationship* Eric Berne (First published 1964) Ballantine Books

- **Parent**
  A state shaped by how parents (or other authority figures) acted
- **Child**
  A state in which people behave, feel, and think similarly to how they did in childhood.
- **Adult**
  A state in which we exercise judgment

When we communicate we do so from one of these states. Berne argued that effective transactions (i.e. successful communications) must be complementary. For example, if the communication is from Parent to Child, the response must be Child to Parent, or the transaction is 'crossed' resulting in ineffective communication, and it is likely that one or other person will be upset. For example, a Chair who adopts a dominating tone may evoke a childlike response such as obedience or an emotional outburst.

If you find this discussion helpful you may also want to look at the work of S.B. Karpman on Drama Triangles which describe a pattern of conflict. People tend to take on different roles such as Persecutor, Rescuer and Victim. Such dynamics can be found between Chair and Chief Executive, with third parties drawn in to complete the destructive triangle.

Self-awareness or support from others can help you identify and break such patterns. Acey Choy explored how to change the dynamics of a drama triangle to a Winner's Triangle by developing awareness of different (more adult) ways of reacting. You can find more details in SECTION 7.

These different analytical lenses can help us understand why we respond as we do. You might like to look again at your preferences on the earlier spectrums in SECTION 3 and ask yourself why you might be attracted to that particular approach. It may meet your own needs. Does it help bring out the best in your CEO? Most crucially does it meet the needs of the organisation you serve?

Strategies for action

These insights suggest the following may be helpful strategies for Chairs:

Practice self-reflection, encourage feedback to help you become aware of your own blind spots.

Clarify roles, responsibilities and boundaries to create a greater sense of security and confidence.

Trust our feelings – they provide important insights about our emotions which are finely attuned to our social environment, subliminally registering others' moods and non-verbal cues. So if we have a 'gut feeling' of unease it may be worth pausing to reflect on the underlying dynamic it may signify.

Be alert to the emotions of the CEO and how they are affecting their behaviour. Excessive anxiety can be crippling. What can you do to reduce anxiety? Aim to create the conditions most conducive to them giving of their best. For example if the CEO's trust or confidence has been damaged by a fractious relationship – with you or a former Chair – you will need to make it safe for them to trust again.

Encourage sharing of feelings to identify unspoken anxiety – or draw attention to the lack of anxiety about a significant decision. 'I am sensing that you are not comfortable with this – do you want to talk about that?' is a useful opener.

Pay attention to where you are in the relationship. At the beginning you will need to spend more time getting to know each other, and exploring what makes you both feel safe enough to work well together. If you have a new CEO do not assume that what you have done before will continue to work for you. You need to start afresh. Transitions are a time of particular vulnerability. It is not unknown for a new Chair to trigger the departure of a CEO.

Learn to ask good questions. The framing of questions can help make the difference between a positive and a negative atmosphere. Seemingly innocent questions can be perceived as a parent talking to a child. Compare *Why don't you do it this way?* with *How are you thinking of doing it?*[3] Try to balance advocacy with inquiry. As Peter Senge highlights, an excess of advocacy can feel like telling whereas an excess of questioning can feel like interrogation.

"I've learnt it's better to ask my CEO 'how are you getting on with xx' rather than 'what are you doing about xx'." IRENE KOHLER

Consider a coach or mentor

A coach and or a mentor can enhance and support your professional development. Good coaches or mentors will provide a framework for your discussions without dictating content, so that the agenda is yours to set, creating a space for you to 'unpack' the things about your role that are really troubling or exciting you.

Coaching and mentoring provide a safe, non-judgmental setting in which you can explore the opportunities and difficulties you are facing, test out the scenarios and options for dealing with them as well as potential consequences.

To explore these ideas further see our *Further reading and resources* section

"The discipline of mental models starts with turning the mirror inward; learning to unearth our internal pictures of the world, to bring them to the surface and hold them rigorously to scrutiny. It also includes the ability to carry on 'learningful' conversations that balance inquiry and advocacy, where people expose their own thinking effectively and make that thinking open to the influence of others[4]. PETER SENGE

---

3 Example from Warren Berger https://hbr.org/2014/07/5-common-questions-leaders-should-never-ask
4 *The Fifth Discipline The Art and Practice of The Learning Organization.* Peter M Senge (First published 1990) Random House

WHEN THINGS GO WRONG
SECTION FIVE

When things go wrong

WHAT ARE YOUR OPTIONS?

SIGNS THAT THE CHAIR-CEO RELATIONSHIP IS IN TROUBLE

- There have been some unpleasant 'surprises', that you feel you should have been alerted to earlier.
- You are not operating as a team. Your opposite number doesn't seem to be able to find the time to talk or meet. Worse, you have come to dread talking to him or her.
- You doubt the explanations you are being offered, or feel that the information provided is not the whole picture.
- There are mutterings among the board or from staff.
- You know something is wrong but it feels too big or difficult to tackle.
- The situation is causing you or your CEO anxiety.
- You are intruding on the CEO's space by making direct requests of staff.
- You have failed to undertake or complete the CEO's appraisal.

We know that the relationship between Chair and CEO doesn't always go well, for a variety of reasons.

This section simply offers some high level guidance and signposting to further help, recognising that unpicking and resolving the particular problems you face will be unique to you and your situation.

First and foremost is a timely acknowledgement that the relationship with your CEO is in difficulty. It does not help to ignore or deny the warning signs and your own unease. Resolve to act, as the problem is highly unlikely to resolve itself.

Once you have recognised this there are only a few courses of action:

- choose a process of reconciliation
- find a way for your CEO to exit (with good grace)
- decide that you will relinquish your role.

We would encourage Chairs to explore first what needs to be done to sustain or repair the relationship with the CEO.

It is not always immediately obvious what the heart of the problem is. When things are not going well, it might be helpful for you to consider what you are doing that may be helping or hindering, and whether some of the factors described in SECTION 4 might be affecting the relationship.

Consider the following questions:

- Are the areas of dispute between you really important or a sideshow? What is driving the disagreements and can those factors be mitigated by actions by you? By those of other trustees?

- Does your CEO need and want external help and support (ACEVO offers members a CEO in Crisis service)

- Is there a genuine misunderstanding?

- Is there a fundamental disagreement about strategy, values, organisational culture?

- Is the CEO really responsible for the current issues or does the responsibility go wider?

- Could mediation be productive, or at least worth trying? Seemingly irreparable relationship breakdowns can be resolved in this way

- Do you believe that the relationship can be repaired or is it permanently damaged?

There are times when a neutral third party can help Chair and CEO find the way forward in a disagreement, whether it is just a sticking point or a serious dispute. The total confidentiality of the process provides the opportunity for both Chair and CEO to speak freely, to identify the root cause(s) of the problem, and to find a mutually agreeable solution. A written agreement/action plan can then be shared with the board if both the Chair and the CEO agree to that.

Things to make sure you consider

- Make sure that the process and timing of what you do is, as far as possible, agreed in advance and is logged and accessible if required

- Keep your trustees informed but ensure confidentiality. There may be a time when you need to alert the CEO to the fact that what is being shared with you in confidence will have to be shared with the board even if this may dent the mutual trust which has been established between you and the CEO, for example, where there are risks for the organisation

- Decide which of your (and your board's) questions need external professional input, for example in relation to finance, employment and charity law

- Be measured, don't rush to a solution.

Difficulties or disputes with your CEO can be demanding, both intellectually and emotionally. Think about what support you need. It is helpful to have external support or the 'wise counsel' of someone who has seen it, been there and can offer the supportive outsider perspective. If you choose to pursue this, talk to other Chairs, seek recommendations. It may take time to find a person who suits you. All Chairs can benefit from help and advice; do see it as a strength to seek it.

Whatever the outcome, reflect on it with the aim of capturing useful learning for you, your trustees and your relationships with the current and future CEO.

INSIGHTS FROM RESEARCH
SECTION SIX

Insights from research

In this section we highlight writing and research concerning the Chair-CEO relationship we think will be most helpful to Chairs interested in this key relationship.

An overview of the literature
Most of the research has been conducted in the private sector with only a few researchers dealing specifically with the charitable and non-profit sectors. It is also a relatively under-researched area.

This can be explained in part by the fact that governance research tends to be dominated by the U.S. where it is less common for the role of Chair and CEO to be held by two different people.

There is a lot of focus on how the relationship should work rather than how it actually does work. There is also a lot of emphasis on setting boundaries between the two roles with little exploration of context or psychology. If you wish to know more about the research please see the literature review on our website conducted by Hilary Barnard.

How do we judge a Chair-CEO relationship?
A report by the NHS Institute for Innovation and Improvement on the relationship between Chairs and Chief Executives in the NHS[5] provides a helpful description of a relationship that is fit for purpose. The relationship:

- Ensures that the joint Chair-CEO leadership role is fulfilled successfully
- Responds well to changing external circumstances and requirements
- Enables the board to operate successfully
- Enables the organisation to operate successfully.

---

5 NHS Institute for Innovation and Improvement (2009) – Understanding the Relationship between Chairs and Chief Execs in the NHS p.5

Interestingly there is a lack of hard evidence demonstrating that a good relationship drives organisational performance – although poor relationships may be associated with poor performance. This is nonetheless a common working assumption and one we share.

What helps achieve a good Chair-CEO relationship?
The literature suggests a wide range of answers as well as some recurring themes.

Trust

Trust is often mentioned as an important element of a successful relationship. Dietz and Den Hartog[6] suggest trust is characterised by four elements:

- **Ability** – perception of leadership competence in doing their job or fulfilling their role

- **Benevolence** – that is their concern for others beyond their own needs: their ability to show care and compassion

- **Integrity** – their trustworthiness as someone who adheres to principles of fairness and honesty while avoiding hypocrisy

- **Predictability** – their behaviour is consistent or regular over time.

For more on trust see discussion of M. Hiland's work on page 61.

Candour and independence of thought

O'Toole and Bennis[7] highlight that leaders need to:

- Tell the truth
- Be willing to admit mistakes
- Share information openly
- Support transparency
- Seek information from multiple sources and not merely rely on what they were told by their close advisors
- Reward contrarians and so avoid group think
- Protect whistleblowers
- Be candid in their dealings with followers.

Agreeing boundaries

The Kakabadses[8] highlight the importance of delineating boundaries. The NHS Institute also highlights the importance but argues that allocating and clarifying roles are not sufficient.

They suggest that irrespective of stated role content, in practice roles will be negotiated explicitly and implicitly by those occupying them. Citing Goss they suggest *Successful leadership pairs show high levels of explicit reflection on divisions of responsibility, mutual strengths and weaknesses and other features of their working relationship.*

Meeting each other's expectations

Walton outlines what Chairs and CEOs value in each other:

WHAT CHAIRS VALUE IN CEOS	WHAT CEOS VALUE IN CHAIRS
Competence	Good at listening
Authenticity	Credibility
Willingness to learn	Together – status equivalence

Sonnenfeld, Kusin and Walton[9] highlight what the CEO wants of the board (and therefore of the Chair too):

- Focus more on the risks that are crucial to the enterprise
- Do your homework
- Bring broad relevant knowledge to the table
- Do more to challenge strategy constructively
- Make succession less, not more, disruptive to operations.

---

6 Dietz and Den Hartog (2006) – Measuring Trust Inside Organisations, Personnel Review Vol 35, Issue 5 Six Disciplines of Chairs
7 O'Toole, J and Bennis, W (2009) – What's needed next: A culture of candour, HBR, Vol 87 No 6 pp54 and pages 56-61
8 Andrew Kakabadse and Nada Kakabadse – Leading the Board: the six disciplines of world-class chairmen (2007)
9 Jeffrey Sonnenfeld, Melanie Kusin and Elise Walton – What CEOs Really Think of Their Boards, HBR, April 2013, pages 98-106

What hinders?
Dominance
Hossack[10] for example highlights the danger of both an over-dominant Chair who meddles and undermines the CEO and of a passive and weak Chair.

He points out: *'a passive and weak chair can be equally dangerous. Contentious issues are swept under the carpet and left unresolved... While a weak chair can seem to make the CEO's life easier, in the end it leaves the CEO to deal with the many different views and factions on the board, ultimately consuming time and making closure on decisions more difficult.'*

Jennifer Sundberg, managing director of Board Intelligence, a consultancy, drew a contrast between the "single intelligence" model of an all-powerful chief executive and the "swarm intelligence" that can operate very successfully in nature[11].

Complexity
Rob Paton suggests that complexities explain why good and capable people sharing the same commitment often end up frustrated and at cross purposes[12].

Behaviour
"The Walker report on governance in the UK's financial sector, for example, recently concluded: 'principal deficiencies related much more to patterns of behaviour than to organisation' (p12). A particular concern... was how non-executives could provide productive challenge without being regarded as disruptive or becoming isolated.

"The appropriate balance, Walker claimed, requires attention to the culture and style of the board – matters that require exceptional board leadership skills from the chairman."[13]

---

10 Together at the top: the critical relationship between the Chairman and the CEO, Ivey Business Journal, January/February 2006 (Hossack – President Mercer Delta Canada)
11 Quoted in Stefan Stern – Effective conversation is vital to success, FT, 14 May 2015
12 Rob Paton (2000) – Effective Governance of Non Profit Organisations, BNAC
13 Quoted in Rob Goffee and Gareth Jones – Why boards go wrong, Management Today, 1 September 2011

Rob Goffee and Gareth Jones observe "The human dynamics at work in the boardroom are acknowledged as important but under investigated."[14]

Other

The NHS Institute for Innovation and Improvement report on the relationship between Chairs and Chief Execs in the NHS provides its own list of pitfalls and challenges:[15]

- Clashes of personality
- Conflict caused by lack of clarity of roles (e.g. micromanagement by the Chair)
- Constraints on non-executive time and energy not enabling confusion over roles to be worked out
- Unresolved conflict which becomes irreconcilable.

Approaches to managing this relationship

Stewart[16] describes five different roles of board Chair in relation to CEO:

- **Partner** Sharing management of the organisation
- **Executive** Directs or forbids action
- **Mentor** Influences CEO's behaviour to positive effect
- **Consultant** Waits to be approached by CEO for advice
- **Distant** Chairing meetings and attending obligatory external meetings.

Mary Hiland's[17] study of 32 U.S. non-profit Chair-CEO relationships explores what distinguishes good and great Chair-CEO relationships. She identified three aspects: interactions between the pair, levels of trust and the focus of the work.

---

14 Why boards go wrong, Management Today, 1 September 2011
15 NHS Institute for Innovation and Improvement (2009) – Understanding the Relationship between Chairs and Chief Execs in the NHS p.6
16 Stewart, R. (1991) Chairman and chief executive: An exploration of their relationship. Journal of Management Study, 28, 5, 511-27
17 Mary Hiland – The Board Chair-Executive Director Dynamic, Journal for Nonprofit Management 2008

INTERACTION

She identified five types of interpersonal dynamics between Chair and CEO:

- **Facts sharing** – One-way giving
- **Ideas sharing** – (e.g. brainstorming and problem solving)
- **Knowledge sharing** – Learning/coaching interaction
- **Feelings sharing** – (e.g. support, appreciation)
- **Give and take** – (e.g. adaptation to other person's style).

The more diverse the interactions between Chair and CEO, the greater the levels of trust. It was the quality of the interactions that mattered not the quantity.

TRUST

Hiland identifies three types of trust

- **Weak trust** is based on a cost benefit calculation, motivated by the extent of punishments and/or rewards.

- **Moderate or knowledge-based trust** results from knowing each other to an extent that facilitates predictability. Chairs and executives gained confidence in each other's competence, showed respect, communicated effectively, and honoured agreements and commitments.

  The executive's willingness to be vulnerable and the board chair creating safety for the executive also exemplified behaviours that built knowledge-based trust.

- **Strong or identification-based trust** results from going beyond knowing each other to identifying with each other. It is built less on predictability of behaviour than on the internalization of each other's preferences.

FOCUS OF WORK

She identified three areas for the focus of work: Managing, Planning, Leading.

The most successful pairs had diverse interactions, the highest level of trust and were engaged in leadership.

Elise Walton identifies three major themes for the working relationship: chemistry, helpful framework, supportive context[18].

GOOD CHEMISTRY

- Frequent and open communications; Chair-CEO relationship "seen not as a bottleneck but as an enabler of communication."
- Reciprocity and consideration
- Close but not personal
- Key interpersonal values.

A CLEAR FRAMEWORK

- Shared commitment to corporate wellbeing
- Defined but adaptable roles
- Effective processes
- Leadership transition strategy.

SUPPORTIVE CONTEXT IS

- A strong and supportive board
- A strong and accessible management team
- The right culture.

A Marriage Made in Heaven by Penelope Gibbs[19] is based on 16 in-depth interviews with Chairs and CEOs. Themes she highlights include good recruitment; communication; roles and expectations; tenure; interaction with other senior managers; challenge, tension and conflict; and friendship and chemistry.

---

18 Elise Walton – Chairmanship: The Effective Chair-CEO Relationship: Insight from the Boardroom, Millstein Centre for Corporate Governance and Performance, Yale University, February 2011
19 A Marriage Made in Heaven – The relationship between Chairs and Chief Executives, P. Gibbs (2011)

FURTHER RESOURCES
SECTION SEVEN

Further resources
AND READING

ACEVO

ACEVO is an important source of information and support for your CEO. We highlight here resources that may be helpful for Chairs too.

Leading the CEO and Chair to Effective Governance
ACEVO (revised 2012) explores the Chair-CEO relationship and has a whole section dedicated to CEO appraisal. It includes examples of CEO role descriptions, a selection of appraisal tools and case studies and a useful role analysis exercise. It also includes a section on *The CEO and Chair in crisis – positive steps for recovery.*

ACEVO also publishes an annual pay survey.

ACEVO's CEO in Crisis service is for CEOs, designed to help when their relationship with the Chair has broken down and they need support in trying to repair the relationship or they believe their job is at risk and want to understand their rights and options. The service is available to full members of ACEVO who have been in membership for three months or more.

NCVO

Good Governance: The Chair's Role
Dorothy Dalton NCVO 2006

Appraising the CEO: 360° profiling
Free on the NCVO/KnowHowNonProfit website
http://knowhownonprofit.org/leadership/role/chiefexecutive/appraising-the-ceo-3600-profiling

The Chief Executive's Relationship with Trustees
Free on the NCVO website
http://knowhownonprofit.org/leadership/role/chiefexecutive/copy2_of_trustees

Lost in Translation – a complete guide to chair/chief executive partnerships
T Akpeki and M Maretich NCVO 2006

Mediation and dispute resolution

There are a number of organisations specialising in dispute resolution through mediation including:

CEDR
http://www.cedr.com

ACAS
http://www.acas.org.uk

Civil Mediation Council
http://www.cmcregistered.org/
Holds a list of registered practitioners

Professional Mediators Association
http://www.professionalmediator.org/
Holds a list of registered practitioners

Further reading

ACADEMIC LITERATURE

See the reading list compiled by Hilary Barnard on our website.

PSYCHOLOGY OF THE RELATIONSHIP

See the briefings by Marcus Page on our website.

PUBLICATIONS

Beneath the surface and around the table: exploring group dynamics in boards
Wendy Reid in *Non-profit governance: Innovative perspectives and approaches* edited by Chris Cornforth and William A Brown, (2014) Routledge.

Emotional Intelligence
Daniel Goleman, (1995) Bantam Books.

I'm OK, You're OK
Thomas Anthony Harris, (1969) Galahad Books.

Games People Play: The Psychology of Human Relationships
Eric Berne, (1964) Ballantine Books.

Fairy tales and script drama analysis
Stephen Karpman MD, (1968) in Transactional Analysis Bulletin 26 (7): 39-43.

The Winner's Triangle
Acey Choy M Ed (1990), Transactional Analysis Journal.

A More Beautiful Question: The Power of Inquiry to Spark Breakthrough
Warren Berger, (2014) Bloomsbury.

The Fifth Discipline: The Art and Practice of The Learning Organization
Peter M Senge, (First published 1990) Random House.

A Marriage Made in Heaven – The relationship between Chairs and Chief Executives
P Gibbs, (2011) available as a free download on the Clore Social Leadership Programme website http://www.cloresocialleadership.org.uk/penelope-gibbs

CONCLUSIONS
SECTION EIGHT

Conclusions

There is no easy formula for achieving a productive relationship between Chair and CEO. It will take time, effort and readjustment to find the right balance for your unique partnership. Nor will it remain static. There will likely be highs and lows, joys and frustrations, and successes as well as disappointments. The relationship and how you approach it will need to be flexible according to the changing needs of your organisation, your CEO, and yourself. It will need and deserves your consistent attention.

The best Chairs relish the opportunity to learn and keep learning. This willingness to learn and adapt is crucial and includes the ability to recognise when your approach may not be helping.

In this guide we have offered you a range of different ways to think about the relationship: looking at what is needed at different stages; exploring how to find a balance by contrasting approaches to key dimensions; offering some frameworks to help you understand your own thoughts and emotions; and highlighting insights from research.

Whatever balance you strike, your shared aim is to provide leadership to the organisation focusing the energy and effort of its people on achieving its agreed mission.

INTERVIEWEES
SECTION NINE

Interviewees

Our interviewees included current and former Chairs and CEOs. They range from those new to leadership roles to those highly experienced. Between them they have led a number of household name charities (including the Royal Opera House, ChildLine, Clic Sargent, the Scouts Association) as well as less well known, though no less important ones.

They also represent different types of organisations: frontline, advisory and support organisations; local, national and international; from an organisation with fewer than ten staff to ones with tens, hundreds and thousands of staff. This helped give us a richness of perspectives.

We were also pleased to interview Martin Farrell of Get 2 the Point who supports CEOs referred from ACEVO's CEOs in Crisis service and who was able to draw on his wide range of experience.

On the next page we list the Chairs we interviewed, with their current or most recent organisation chaired.

LIST OF INTERVIEWEES
AND THEIR CURRENT OR MOST RECENT ORGANISATION CHAIRED

Pelham Allen
Bloodwise

Bishop John Arnold
CAFOD and Oxford and Cambridge Catholic Education Board

Robert Arnott
Cardinal Hume Centre

Carole Easton
Young Minds

Chris Freed
Voluntary Action Lewisham

Beryl Hobson
NCT (Former Chair)

Duncan Ingram
Children's Trusts

Jo Jowett
ECM Britain

Irene Kohler
Swan Advocacy

Julia Lever
The Makaton Charity

Graham Meek
King's College Hospital Foundation Trust (Former Acting Chair)

Gerald Oppenheim
The Camden Society

Sarah Phillips
Demelza Hospice Care for Children

Claire Ryan
Daybreak

Hilary Sears
MS Society and Kids

Angela Style
Endometriosis UK

Derek Twine
Bradford Cathedral Council

Rebecca Weinberg
St Gemma's Hospice

We have also included some quotes from CEOs and Chairs who we do not list here.

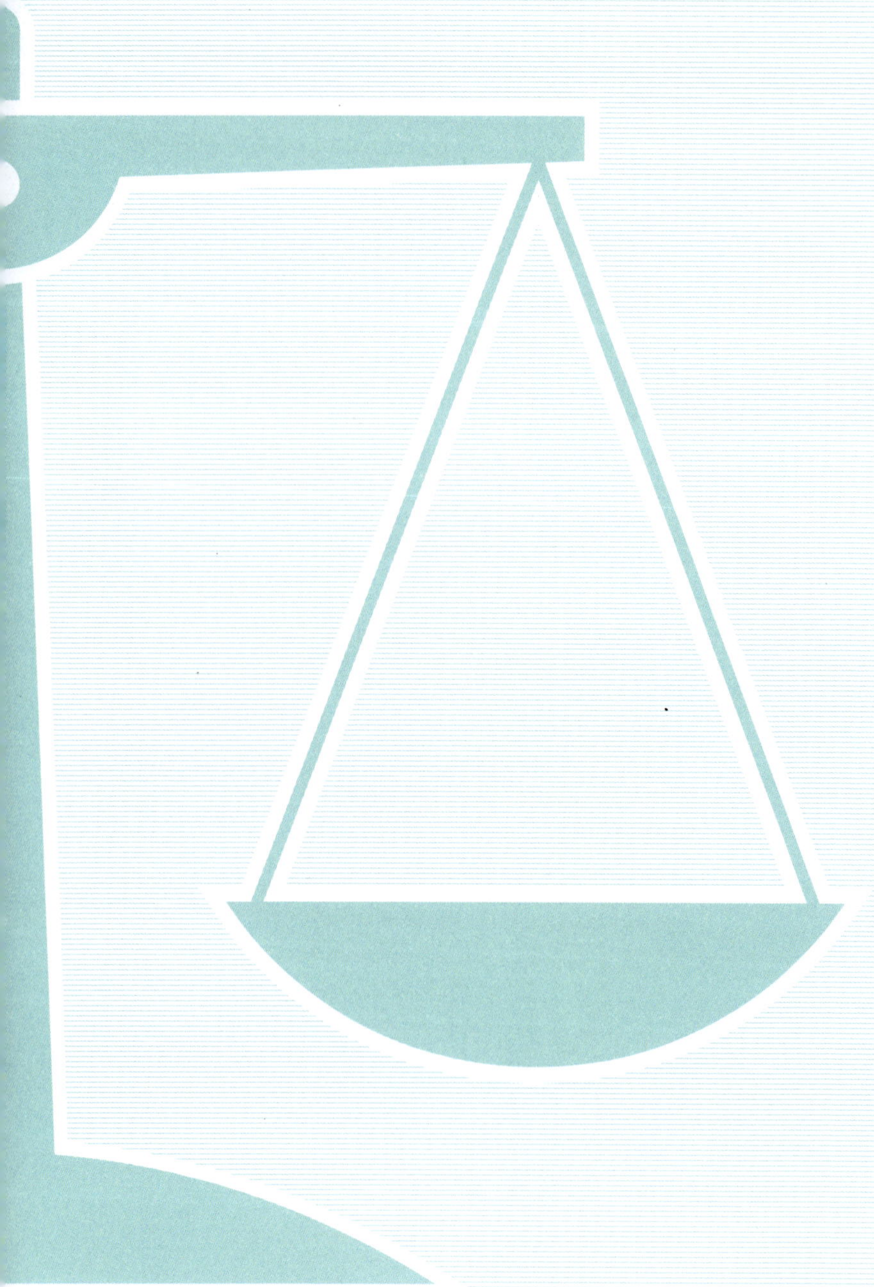

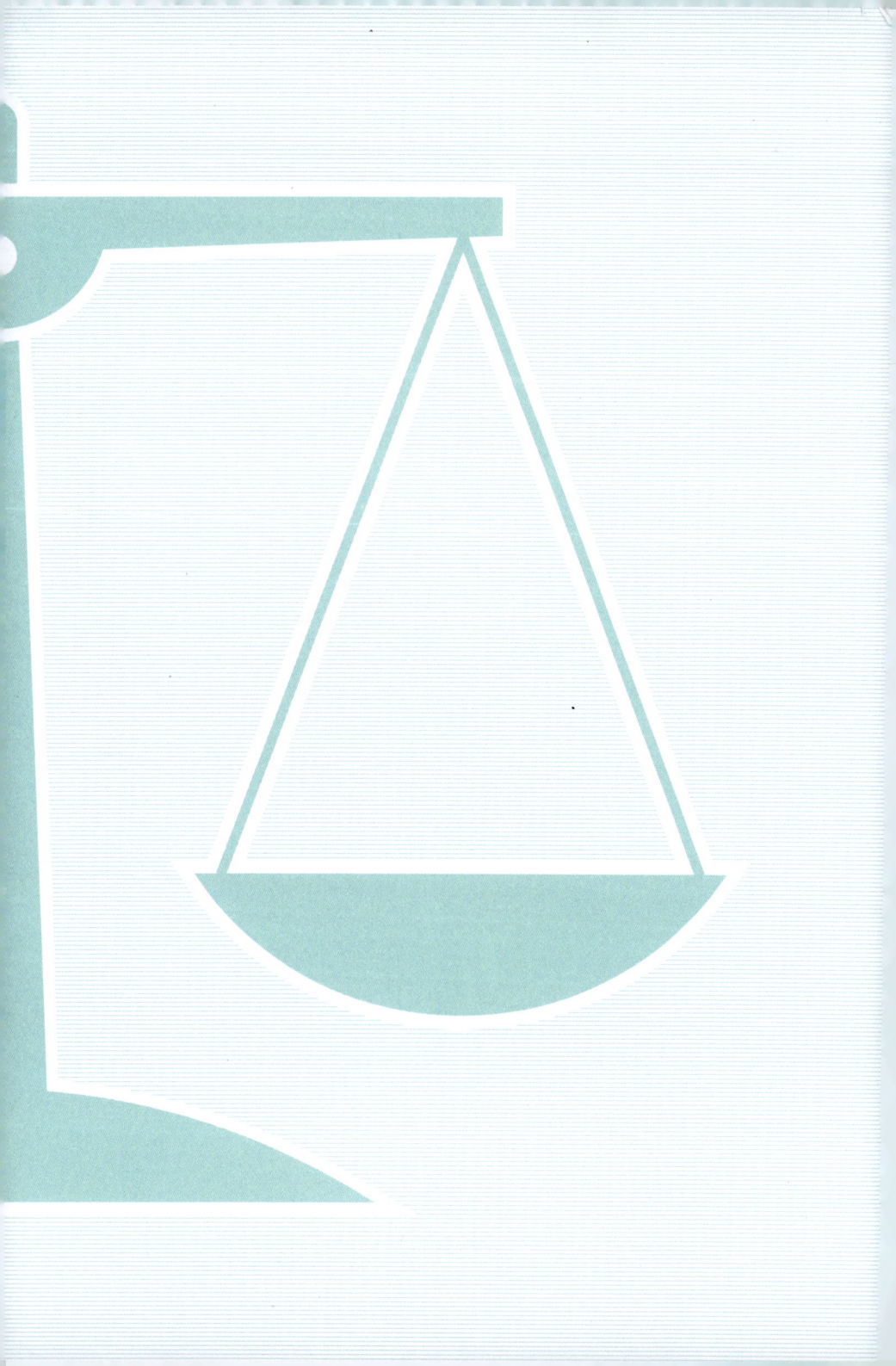